Around the Churches
of
The South Hams
II

Walter Jacobson

With love and especial thanks for Page 4!

Walter

GW00673462

OBELISK PUBLICATIONS

ALSO BY THE AUTHOR

Around the Churches of East Devon
Around the Churches of Exeter
Around the Churches of The Teign Valley
Around the Churches of The South Hams

OTHER BOOKS ABOUT THIS AREA

The South Hams in Colour, *Chips Barber*
Walks in the South Hams, *Brian Carter*
Villages of the South Hams, *John Legge*
Dart Country, *Deryck Seymour*
Around & About Hope Cove and Thurlestone, *Chips Barber*
Around & About Burgh Island and Bigbury Bay, *Chips Barber*
Around & About Salcombe, *Chips Barber*
Newton Ferrers and Noss Mayo, *Chips Barber*
Beesands and Hallsands of Yesteryear, *Cyril Courtenay*
The Great Little Totnes Book, *Chips Barber*
The Ghosts of Totnes, *Bob Mann*
Walks in the Totnes Countryside, *Bob Mann*
The Ghosts of Berry Pomeroy Castle, *Deryck Seymour*
Place-Names in Devon, *Chips Barber*
An A to Z of Devon Dialect, *Chips Barber*
Haunted Pubs in Devon, *Sally and Chips Barber*
Ghastly and Ghostly Devon, *Sally and Chips Barber*
Murders and Mysteries in Devon, *Ann James*

We have over 170 Devon-based titles; for a list of current books please send SAE to
2 Church Hill, Pinhoe, Exeter, EX4 9ER or telephone (01392) 468556

Acknowledgements

All photographs supplied by Walter Jacobson and Chips Barber.
Front cover: Stokenham Church; back cover: ruins of South Huish Church by Chips Barber.
Thanks to Rita Dunkley for her map of the South Hams recording the sites of churches in
Volumes I and II.

First published in 2001 by
Obelisk Publications, 2 Church Hill, Pinhoe, Exeter, Devon
Designed and Typeset by Sally Barber
Printed in Great Britain

CONTENTS

INTRODUCTION

IN publishing a first book, *Around the Churches of the South Hams*, it became apparent that there was material to fill a second. During the autumn of 2000 I had the pleasure of visiting more of the fine churches in the area, and their stories are included here.

The new book includes other churches situated south of the main A38 road between Exeter and Plymouth, and some are set in the romantic heights of South Dartmoor, tracing back to their source the rivers which have carved the valleys and formed the picturesque estuaries of the South Hams.

In this mainly rural setting, the subjects chosen are again all parish churches – not from an Anglican preference, but because historically they reach back to the days when there were no denominations.

In that respect, I believe these ancient buildings belong to all Christians, and indeed can be regarded as shrines by all parishioners aware of a mutual heritage. Once they were the meeting place for the whole community, and today they are again being used as welcoming social centres as well as places of worship.

Perhaps what is most fascinating is that the stories of the parishes are so different, dependent as they are upon people, and so far it is true that no human being is the clone of another.

In compiling each article, I have relied upon numerous sources, many of them referred to in the text, and I am most indebted to the Devon Studies Library in Exeter. Where options occur, I have presented different points of view.

This is now the fifth book on churches printed by Obelisk Publications. Originally most of these articles – and many others – were printed in Exeter's *Express and Echo*, and I am grateful to Sandra George of the Devon Historic Churches Trust, who entrusted me with the task in the first place.

ST THOMAS OF CANTERBURY CHURCH, DODBROOKE

DODBROOKE Parish Church is one of seven in the Exeter Diocese dedicated to Archbishop Thomas Becket, murdered by four knights in Canterbury Cathedral in 1170. There is a theory that one of the knights, a Devonian, William de Tracy, owned land in this parish, and as part of his penance for the murder rebuilt the church and changed its dedication to St Thomas (he was made a saint in 1173).

Another conjecture is that a new church was built by the lords of Dodbrooke's Manor in Becket's honour at the request of Henry III, whose grandfather Henry II had instigated the archbishop's murder with the famous remark overheard by the four zealous knights: "Who will rid me of this turbulent priest?"

Henry III wanted Dodbrooke's priest to intercede for his grandfather's soul in purgatory, and by way of reward granted the parish the privilege of a market and assize of beer in 1257.

Out of the mists of those distant days comes the tale of Matthew Fitz-John and his 40 "merrie men", who paid a penalty to the lord of the manor for throwing down a pillory in Dodbrooke.

It is interesting that Devonians quietly disobeyed Henry VIII's order that patrons of all English churches dedicated to Thomas should replace him with another saint.

There was almost certainly a Saxon chapel here founded by a thane named Dodda. In Edward the Confessor's time, the manor was apparently held by Brictric, Thane of Gloucester, who had jilted Matilda, daughter of Count Baldwin of Flanders, before her marriage to William I (the Conqueror).

After the Conquest, Matilda, whose fame was established in creating the Bayeux Tapestry, took revenge by confiscating Brictric's many Devon manors, but here it seems that she relented and Dodbrooke Manor passed to Brictric's widow (after his execution).

Later it came to the Lord Fitz-Rualds, who probably built the first Norman church. The font comes from that time, about 1170, by coincidence also the date of Becket's murder.

The Champernownes later attached Dodbrooke to their other lands in Modbury and Dartington and may have been responsible for the mainly 15th century structure of the present church. The north aisle was originally named after the family, but it fell into disrepair and was replaced by the parishioners in 1887.

At the west end of the aisle an Oddfellows window was being repaired when I visited the church. Warden of 40 years Mr Reg Angel explained that the window was a unique feature visited by Oddfellow members from far and wide.

The fine mediaeval rood and parclose screens were carefully restored in the 19th century with expert carving by Henry Hems. Installed in the north arcade are pillars and arches from the South Huish Church, which fell into ruin in 1869.

The famous name of John Wolcot appears in the parish baptism register on 9 May 1738. After an extraordinary career as an ordained Anglican priest and a surgeon in Cornwall and the West Indies, he became a leading satirist of his age with the pseudonym Peter Pindar.

His pen spared nobody, and King George III and his courtiers were sitting targets. Referring to his childhood home in Kingsbridge, he once wrote: "I love every mouse in that old-fashioned house…"

In more reflective mood he wrote:

"Care to our coffin adds a nail, no doubt;
And every grin so merry, draws one out."

When Wolcot eventually succumbed to a coffin, he was buried on 14 January 1819, in St Paul's Church, Covent Garden.

ST MARY'S CHURCH, CHARLETON

A SEAT by the entrance of St Mary's Church, given by the Charleton Women's Fellowship in 1976, is well placed for the wonderful view down the valley towards the Kingsbridge Estuary. The name Charleton has been given several interpretations – one is "Churl's farm", another "chief's farm", and a third, which seems most apt, is "rock farm", derived from an old Celtic word meaning "stone".

The reason is that the material for many of the churches and other buildings in the South Hams, including the original 14th century structure of St Mary's itself, was obtained from the slate quarries which were worked at Charleton from the 13th century onwards. The square tower of Dartmouth Castle was also built from stone quarried in the parish in 1488.

Although the screen and other interior features disappeared when the church was rebuilt in 1849–50, the 14th century tower, with its distinctive turret reminiscent of a castle, remains intact.

A visitor of a century ago was told by the sexton that the curfew bell was once housed there on top of the tower, but later transferred to the ringing chamber, where it continued its function to call parishioners home every evening.

Domesday records of "Cheltona" reveal that its revenues were given to Judhael, Lord of Totnes, after the Conquest, and he in turn gave the tithes to support his foundation of Totnes Priory.

The interior is restful, and the ancient south transept has a glorious modern stained glass window depicting Nativity scenes.

There are several nostalgic memorials recalling how the Pax Britannica was maintained by servicemen overseas for the last quarter of the second millennium. Chief of these is the memorial, also in the south transept, to the Rev Thomas Whinyates, 41 years Rector of Charleton, his wife Amy, and their only son Major Thomas Whinyates, who married Catherine, daughter of Admiral Sir Thomas Frankland. The younger couple both died in India in March 1806.

Their five sons and six daughters are also named. Of the sons, two became generals, one a major general, another a rear admiral, and the fifth a Royal Navy commander. Family pride inspired the inscription: "The men were handsome, brave, and strong and all of them fought in battle for their country. The women were beautiful and good and, save one, they all attained to great age."

Col Bill Charter, MC, of the Indian Army, is also remembered as a member of the International Association of Cape Horners (open only to those who have rounded the Horn in sailing vessels), and the plaque quotes the poem Tennyson wrote in a vessel anchored in the Salcombe Estuary:
"I hope to see my Pilot face to face
When I have crossed the bar."

ST CLEMENT'S CHURCH, TOWNSTAL, DARTMOUTH

STANDING steeply 350 feet above the River Dart, St Clement's, Townstal, was the "mother" church of the Port of Dartmouth. Some historians believe that Saxon, or even Celtic, Christians may have worshipped in a wooden chapel here long ago.

After 1066 the Manor of Townstal (or Dunstal), meaning "hill homestead", passed from a Saxon named Ansgor into Norman ownership, eventually coming into the possession of William FitzStephen.

The church was dedicated to St Clement, third successor of St Peter as Bishop of Rome, who was martyred in AD 96. His image was featured in a stained glass window with his anchor emblem – most appropriate for a town so long associated with Britain's maritime history.

The oldest monument in the church is an effigy carved in Purbeck marble. Opinions have differed about whom the recumbent statue is supposed to represent, but the most favoured theory is that it commemorates Isabella de Languire, wife of Willam FitzStephen.

By an agreement officially sanctioned in a document signed by Simon of Apulia, Bishop of Exeter 1214–1223, William FitzStephen bestowed lands and the care of the church upon the Abbot of Torre in Torquay. The condition was that the monks should pray diligently for the safe passage of the souls of William and Isabella.

A new stone church was built in these times, but the people who lived by the riverside became increasingly weary of climbing the steep hill to worship.

When King Edward I visited Dartmouth in 1286, they seized the opportunity to ask his permission to build a church in the port area. The King agreed, but the Abbot of Torre and the Bishop of Exeter did not.

The project went ahead without their consent, however, and the first St Saviour's Church was blessed by a fictitious "Bishop of Damascus". Eventually a new Bishop of Exeter agreed to consecrate the independent church in 1372.

Meanwhile the mysterious death by drowning of the Vicar of Townstal, Richard de Wydcombe, on 13 September 1329 caused consternation. Was it suicide – or even murder?

All services were stopped at St Clement's, except for a midnight Mass at Christmas, until Bishop Grandisson rededicated the building.

The Abbots of Torre held the right to assign vicars for 300 years, and as almost his final act before the abbey was dissolved by Henry VIII in 1539, the last abbot, Simon Rede, appointed himself as incumbent and came to live in Townstal Vicarage.

The church acquired its Purbeck marble font in the 13th century and a finely carved communion table, with images of four seated lions on its legs, in the reign of James I.

When General Thomas Fairfax led the Roundhead troops in 1646 to seize Devon and Cornwall in the Civil War, St Clement's was the chosen stronghold for the Cavaliers, who fired cannon shots from the tower, putting up a stubborn but fruitless resistance against the invaders.

An east window was installed in memory of Sir Henry Paul Seale, Bart., of the Mount Boone estate in the parish, who was MP for Dartmouth 1832–1844.

Sir Henry's second son, Charles, married a Miss Hayne from the neighbouring parish of Blackawton. He died at 33 and was buried in the chancel in 1842, leaving a widow and only child, Charles Seale-Hayne, who was Liberal MP for Ashburton from 1885 until his death in 1903. At one stage he was a member of Gladstone's Cabinet.

Being a bachelor, he decided to leave his fortune of £150,000 to establish the Seale-Hayne Agricultural College near Newton Abbot.

ST MARY'S CHURCH, BERRY POMEROY

ONE of the fairest parishes in England, Berry Pomeroy, with its well-preserved church and haunted ruined castle, has a romantic history to match its peaceful charm.

Since the Norman Conquest manorial rights have been held by just two families – the Pomeroys and the Seymours (Dukes of Somerset).

Ralph de Pomeroi was head of the family which built the church and first manor house, and one of his descendants built the castle, probably in the reign of Edward III (1327–77). Although it fell into decay from the 18th century, the castle in the depth of the woods remains one of Devon's best-kept secrets from tourism.

The crest of the Pomeroys is to be found in old glass in the church, and the family tomb in the chancel is thought to be the resting place of Sir Richard Pomeroy, who died in 1496.

Sir Edward Seymour, first Duke of Somerset, bought the castle from the beleaguered Catholic Pomeroys in the first year of the reign of his nephew, the Protestant King Edward VI, whose mother, Jane Seymour, died soon after his birth.

As Protector during his nephew's minority, Sir Edward tried to placate Catholic families while creating a Protestant nation and promoting the first English Prayer Book; but his rival, the Earl of Warwick, eventually secured his execution in 1552 by forging a warrant from the young King.

There is a striking memorial to his son, also Edward, reclining in armour in the Seymour chapel. He was imprisoned for nine years because he had married the sister of the lovely but unlucky Lady Jane Grey, Queen of England for a short time before her execution in 1554.

The memorial also features his son (third Duke) and son's wife Elizabeth, a Champernowne from the neighbouring parish of Dartington.

The Royal Arms of William and Mary in the church are a reminder that they were welcomed at Berry Pomeroy Castle by Charles (nicknamed "The Proud"), sixth Duke of Somerset, soon after their arrival at Brixham in 1688.

William is thought to have held his first Parliament at Longcombe House in the parish, now known as "Parliament House", en route to the castle.

Evidence of the Seymour link down to the present day is the 1923 window in memory of Algernon, 15th Duke of Somerset, and his wife Susan.

One of Devon's early historians, the Rev John Prince (Vicar 1681–1723), who recorded stories of county families in *The Worthies of Devon*, has a chancel memorial. His long-serving successors were Joseph Fox (Vicar 1723–81) and John Edwards (1781–1834): so three men cared for the parish over 153 years.

Spacious and light, with a fine screen and windows, St Mary's is an historic gem well suited for timeless worship.

ST GEORGE'S CHURCH, DITTISHAM

FRUIT trees flourish in the sheltered valley where St George's Church, Dittisham, stands on a rise, commanding memorable views of the River Dart as it nears the end of its journey from Dartmoor to the sea.

Although under Saxon kings this favoured parish was held by the Diocesan Bishops (stationed at Crediton until 1050, then at Exeter), it was eased from their grasp after 1066 by Sheriff Baldwin, Devon's largest landowner under William the Conqueror.

One of his descendants, Hugh Courtenay, became Lord of the Manor c. 1300, and in 1333 Bishop Grandisson consecrated a new building of local stone, with a longer chancel and additional aisles.

Retained from the old building was the red sandstone font. Three centuries later, when Cromwell's troops invaded the area, the font was buried in a field for safety and dug up and restored to the church only in the 19th century.

The mediaeval pulpit carved in stone is one of 60 of its kind in England, including 11 in Devon, according to J. M. Slader, who adds: "The finest is in Dittisham, gleaming in gold and still retaining its original blue painted figures of John the Baptist and four companions."

Memorials to the Strode family include one to Rector John Strode, who was turned out of his home with his family by "an unruly mob" during the Commonwealth.

They installed a Puritan minister, Edward Tooker, in his place, but Strode survived and returned as rector in 1660, when the monarch was restored. A memorial records his death here in 1670, and Charles II's Arms over the door date from these times.

Across the river from the church, Greenway House was the favourite home of the Gilberts. Their cousin, Sir Walter Raleigh, used to stay and smoked his silver pipe of peace on the "Anchor Stone", with tobacco grown in his colony of Virginia. A more recent occupant of Greenway was novelist Agatha Christie.

A vestry book entry of 17 March 1770, tells how a music master was engaged to improve the psalm singing of the congregation. He was paid £5 per annum from a special rate raised in the parish.

When the Rt Hon Lord Kerr, Viscount Valletort, was Rector 1827–52, he employed one of the great architects of the day, Augustus Pugin, to design four-light windows in the aisles.

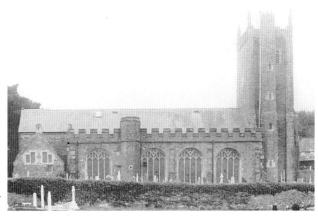

In 1933, to mark the 600th anniversary of the church's rebuilding, a new reredos was dedicated and a fund started for the restoration of the mediaeval screen.

Carved heads of Queen Elizabeth II and her son and heir Prince Charles were placed over the west door to commemorate the Coronation of 1953.

The lovely interior is further enhanced by hassocks embroidered by members of the congregation, featuring the striking red and white colours of St George.

ST PETER'S CHURCH, CORNWORTHY

WITH an interior which lives up to the promise of its fair exterior, St Peter's Church, Cornworthy, has also stood on a hill looking north east towards the River Dart for at least 800 years, as its circular Norman font testifies.

Half a mile west above the village is the elegant gatehouse, all that remains of the priory founded for Augustinian nuns around 1205. It was first mentioned in 1238, when Prioress Hawysia had a business meeting with her tenants.

A successor, Prioress Lady Anastasia, in January, 1277, crossed the Dart for another business meeting with the Prior of Totnes under the yew tree in Littlehempston churchyard – obeying a strict rule which demanded that neither could visit the other's religious house.

Around 1520, however, Bishop Veysey of Exeter scolded the nuns for their lack of religious tone, telling them to take their meals silently together while contemplative lectures were read, not to wear pompous apparel, and "not to receive sojourners without special licence".

The priory, which provided for vicars at the parish church, closed at the general dissolution in 1536, and the field in which the gatehouse remains is now a venue for the annual village pig roast.

An altar made from granite, once part of the priory, was placed in the church when the Lady Chapel was restored in 1968.

Sir Piers Edgcombe, Sheriff of Devon in 1529, whose crest appears in the church, made a passionate but fruitless plea in a letter to Chancellor Thomas Cromwell that the priory be spared. His family had helped in the upkeep of the present church, which took shape about 600 years ago.

A canopied tomb in the sanctuary, with effigies of Sir Thomas Harris and his wife Elizabeth (daughter of Henry Pomeroy) notes that this "worthy gentleman" died in May 1610.

Historian John Prince, Rector of Berry Pomeroy, wrote that the priory lands were bought by William, father of Sir Thomas Harris, who wears the 17th century cap of a Sergeant-at-law. One son, Edward, became Chief Justice of Munster in "Yerlande".

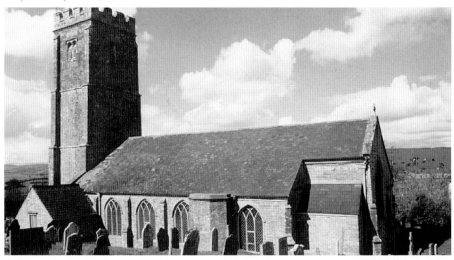

The attractive wall memorial to Lucy Spurway is inscribed: "Being in the 23rd year of her age, resigned her soul into the hands of the gracious Creator, January 8, 1687, and the body was here interred in hope of ye resurrections of ye just."

An all-time Devon record was notched up by the Rev Charles Barter, who was Vicar here for 71 years (1775–1846). His Parish Clerk for 40 of those years, John Tucker, was also the schoolmaster, wrote the parishioners' wills, and read the lessons "in admirable style".

In the light and unspoiled interior, local residents have displayed a book since 1994, recording the parish history and outstanding aspects of modern life.

ST DAVID'S CHURCH, ASHPRINGTON

GUARDING its attractive village on a hill west of the River Dart, Ashprington Church is one of the few in England dedicated to the 6th century Welsh patron, St David.

This has led to conjecture that a chapel was established here in Celtic times 1,600 years ago, and the valued link with the saint was confirmed in 1966, when Bishop Robert Mortimer of Exeter blessed a Lady Chapel Altar containing a piece of stone from the Cathedral Church of St David in Wales.

Matilda, William I's Queen, bestowed the manor to Judhael, Lord of Totnes, who gave the income to the town's cell of French monks, on condition that they prayed for the Queen's soul.

Praised for its simple dignity and good preservation, the Norman font of red sandstone, with honeysuckle design, was set under the tower built about the same time.

The north aisle was added when Thomas Coterell founded a chantry to pray for the souls of his ancestors, the priest's salary to be 106s 8d (£5.33), the poor to receive 4s 4d (22p) annually, and provision to be made for bread, wine, and wax for the Mass.

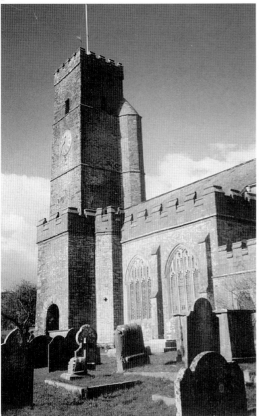

In 1308 Rector Nicholas de Mothaye was dismissed by Bishop Stapeldon for being illiterate and tactless, and the Vicar of Totnes was given temporary care of the parish.

A few years later Bishop Grandisson summoned William, of Hamme, Ashprington, "apparently insane, who calls himself a hermit" to appear before him.

It was recorded on brass that William Somaster, of Pyneford, died in 1589 "and lieth here buried. Christ is my life and Christ my advantage."

A romantic story is related about two families commemorated here, the Pownalls and the Bastards, of Sharpham, a spectacular property bordering the Dart, with gardens designed by Capability Brown.

Capt. Philemon Pownall, a wealthy naval officer, rebuilt Sharpham before being killed in action in 1780, leaving a daughter Jane as heiress.

Young Edward Bastard was so enamoured of the property (and we hope the heiress) that he persuaded Jane to elope with him, "first making practical preparations by hiring all the post horses in the neighbourhood, so that nobody could pursue them."

John Lethbridge, ousted as Rector by the Roundheads, hid in Sharpham Woods for 14 days while his wife and children were evicted from the Rectory. The family fled to Cornwall, where John died in 1655.

Rector for 64 years until his death in 1859, Jacob Ley presided over church repairs. The finely carved Victorian pulpit is in memory of Mrs Mary Carwithen, daughter of Sir Edward Creasy, Chief Justice of Ceylon.

The church guide book informs us that the 700-year-old chalice is the oldest communion vessel still used in any English parish church, and is kept in safety away from the building.

ST MICHAEL AND ALL ANGELS CHURCH, STOKENHAM

STILL a focus for everything (as the Women's Institute *The Devon Village Book* reveals), St Michael and All Angels Church, Stokenham, stands proudly a little above its village on a site which was once a holy well.

A porch notice, in fine calligraphy, announces: "In the beginning, the building of Stokenham's first Parish Church occurred around 1186. The builder was Matthew Fitz Herbert, a devout warrior and courtier, the first lord of the manor of Stokenham."

Earlier, in Saxon times, there is speculation that there may well have been a "minster", or small college of clergy, stationed here.

The present church is a stately building – some call it the Cathedral of the South Hams, rivalling All Saints' Church, Malborough – with a fine tower, an ancient font, and a well preserved 15th century screen.

There was a Royal connection with the manor, once adjacent to the church, and the parish was described by Bishop Grandisson as a "lucrative" living.

In 1309 Edward II is reported to have allowed the squire's widow to hold the manor in dower with reversion to Rolf de Monthermer and his two sons – the King's nephews.

In the British Museum there is a letter of 1405 sent to King Henry IV from Thomas Fitz Alan, Earl of Arundel, requesting him to bestow this rich parish on Adam Davenport, Chancellor of the Queen of Portugal (the King's sister). Edward Prentys, who had been rector, resigned in favour of the candidate "of these great people", but was eventually reinstated in 1422.

In 1547, when the Collegiate Church of Crediton was dissolved, Dean George Mason was offered the wealthy living as compensation.

Exactly a century later, Rector Jonas Styles, expelled by the Roundheads, escaped to Padua where he became a doctor of medicine. He died, a year after being reinstated, in 1662. Buried in the churchyard is Katherine, daughter of Royalist William Randall. She was killed when their home was attacked by Parliamentarian troops.

The numerous monuments, which are given full coverage in the church guide, include those in the south chapel of the Holdsworth family, of Widdicombe House, who had a long association with the parish. Memorials include those to Charles Holdsworth, who was the incumbent and died in 1829, and Arthur, killed in action in 1916.

When the parish was evacuated in 1943 to provide a training ground for American troops, the church itself was damaged by a "friendly" shell.

Recent additions, showing the skills of parishioners, include the striking model of the church, which at the press of a button lights up and plays the sound of organ and bells; and the 300 kneelers representing many devoted hours of fine tapestry.

Most welcoming, too, are the 20-plus photos of dogs in the porch, presented in gratitude for the parishioners' generosity to the cause of Guide Dogs for the Blind.

ST PETER'S CHURCH, STOKE FLEMING

RENOWNED for centuries as a landmark for mariners, St Peter's Church, Stoke Fleming, is thought to have been an early foundation. The church may have been at the centre of a fortification which stood the villagers in good stead from the attacks of marauding seafarers from Scandinavia or the Continent.

One recorded invasion on the coast below came from Brittany in 1404 and was repelled by a force from Dartmouth.

The name Fleming is derived from a Flemish knight, Flanderensis de Stok (anglicised to Sir Richard Fleming), who as lord of the manor was one of the church's first patrons. It seems that he served with Richard Coeur de Lion at the Crusades.

The circular red sandstone Norman font was retained when

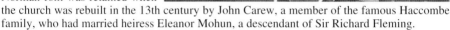

the church was rebuilt in the 13th century by John Carew, a member of the famous Haccombe family, who had married heiress Eleanor Mohun, a descendant of Sir Richard Fleming.

The effigy now kept in the tower arch is believed to represent Lady Eleanor.

Connoisseurs have long been fascinated by the elegant brass, one of the oldest in the Westcountry, of John Corp and his granddaughter, Elyenor. A merchant colleague of John Hawley (see St Saviour's Church, Dartmouth), he died in 1350. Elyenor lived on until 1391.

The brass to Elias Newcomen (Rector 1600–1614) contains the famous punning quotation: "Elias old lies here entombed in grave, but New-com-in to Heaven's habitation."

His great-grandson, Thomas Newcomen, was the Dartmouth inventor who won lasting fame by producing the first practical steam engine, used primarily to pump water from mine shafts.

Elias' successor as rector was Richard Reynolds, formerly chaplain to James I's Queen Anne, who was warned in 1644 that Puritan troops were on their way from Plymouth to seize him.

While he was making his escape dressed as a farmer, he met the would-be captors, who asked him the way to Stoke Fleming. Directing them, he said he "hoped they would secure that old malignant Reynolds."

After much privation, including time spent hiding in a Cornish tin mine, he was restored as Rector in 1660, in his 100th year, and resigned in favour of his son-in-law, John Brooker.

Buried in the churchyard, George Parker Bidder, the mathematical genius (see also St Petrox, Dartmouth), has his memorial in a stained glass window presented by his wife.

The outstanding woodwork of Violet Pinwill, of Ermington, provided the altar; and the pulpit, which was carved when she was 17 in 1891, features a veritable menagerie of animals and birds.

Visitors look again in surprise at the lectern, where the Bible rests on the wings of a large seagull carved in 1984 by Nigel Watson, of Ashburton.

ST JAMES THE GREATER CHURCH, SLAPTON

FIRST impression on entering Slapton village, perched above the extensive beach and the freshwater Ley, is a ruined tower standing apart from and above the spire of St James the Greater Church.

The tower is all that remains of a chantry that was raised in 1373 by Sir Guy de Brian – the most celebrated of a succession of knights of that name, who was a standard bearer of Edward III at the Battle of Crecy and one of the first Knights of the Garter.

John Leland, the much quoted 16th century writer, observed: "Slaptoune is a praty college towards the shore, almost in the middle way betwixt Dartmouth and Saltcombe haven. Guy Brienne founded it."

Of the six priests and four clerks at the college, one priest was deputed to care for the parishioners and their church, which "lapsed in dignity".

Much earlier the manor – and we may assume the building and care of the first stone church – descended from William the Conqueror's time through the hands of the acquisitive Baldwin, Norman Sheriff of Devon, down to the de Brian family c. 1250 or before. After alterations to the building, the high altar was dedicated in 1318 by Bishop Stapeldon.

Apparently hidden in a nearby field to evade the zeal of reformers, a stone with five crosses from this original altar is incorporated in the present altar.

After the chantry's enforced closure in the 16th century, the church was the only centre of worship for rich and poor alike.

Around 1600 Lady Judith Hawkins, from stately Poole House, came to pray. Popular legend tells how two black pages unrolled a red velvet carpet so that she did not soil her feet on the muddy path. She was the wife of Admiral Sir Richard Hawkins, one of the Devon seafaring family, and a stone records her burial here in 1629, seven years after the death of her husband.

Two small figures of the Amerediths, who also lived at Poole House in the 16th century, were discovered during a church restoration in 1905.

Dean Milles of Exeter in a visit c.1750 reported on a wooden Ameredith memorial on the north side of the chancel – a man and a woman kneeling opposite each other with the inscription: "Here lieth the man whose end well brooke his name, a merry death he died; and lived the same."

Another member of a Sidmouth branch of the family, Griffith Ameredith, Sheriff of Exeter 1555, founded a charity to provide shrouds for those condemned to death in the city.

Many Dartmouth people walked to St James Church to hear Nonconformist John Flavel preach after he was expelled from St Saviour's under the Five Mile Act. Eventually that act was repealed, and Flavel's admirers built him a chapel in Dartmouth where he preached for the rest of his days.

Capt Peter Charig, RN, gives a full account of the parishioners' sacrificial role in the Second World War when church and village were vacated to allow the American allies to prepare for the Normandy landing. The church's screens and other valuable items were removed for safety for the duration of the war.

In 1975, after a successful public appeal, the tower ring of five bells was increased to six and blessed by the Bishop of Plymouth.

ST GABRIEL'S CHURCH, STOKE GABRIEL

THE MOST striking feature of Stoke Gabriel Parish Church is its yew tree. An expert, Allen Meredith, refers to it in *The Sacred Yew*, the comprehensive survey (1994) written by Anand

Chetan, of Buckland in the Moor, and Diana Brueton.

Meredith asks: "Why is it one of the most famous yews in the country? Over the centuries many authors have written about it."

There are older specimens in Devon church-yards – notably at Dartington and Bampton (both 1,500 years) and at Kenn and Mamhead (2,000 years). Estimated to be 850 years old, Stoke Gabriel's yew may seem a mere youngster, but it is a fine sight, and could easily have sprung, as often happens, out of the roots of a much older tree destroyed by lightning.

As yews stood on sites sacred to the druids long before the Christians built their churches, they have also been associated with pagan practices, and Stoke Gabriel is no exception. References have been made to the retention of a fertility rite in which couples circle the tree.

A church was already established here in 1073, according to a register of Bishop Osbern.

Local residents view with affection the cobbled walk leading to the door and the 15th century font, screen, and pulpit. The Sandridge chapel has a slate tablet to the wife of one of the Pomeroys, the Norman family who lived in this part of Devon.

Sandridge Barton was the home of the parish's most famous son, John Davis, who was baptised at the font and made his marriage vows at the altar. A contemporary and friend of the Gilberts and Walter Raleigh (see Dittisham), he was the poineer explorer who discovered Hudson Bay. He gave his name to Davis Strait between Greenland and Canada, and when mapping Labrador he named Mt Raleigh after his boyhood friend. In his ship *Desire* he also discovered the Falkland Islands on 14 August 1592.

Among the vicars who have served in this pleasant corner of the widening Dart, for long the centre of a salmon fishing industry, were Finney Benfield, who stayed nearly 50 years, and

"Parson" Neville (Vicar 1881–1916), who is fondly remembered for breaking down a gate obstructing the public footpath to the riverside Duncannon Beach.

In 1985 Vicar John Scholefield pre-sented Mr George Narracott, then 70, with a gold pocket watch upon his completion of 50 years as verger. By that time, members of the Narracott family had held the office of verger from 1440 – totalling 545 years without a break. Surely an item for the *Guinness Book of Records*.

Stone from the Galmpton Creek Quarry in the parish was extracted to build Totnes Church tower in the 15th century.

CHURCH OF ST PAUL DE LEON, STAVERTON

SNOWDROPS in their thousands have heralded spring in the churchyard of St Paul de Leon Church, Staverton, over the centuries. One legend claimed that a first church founded by the Celts 1,400 years ago was dedicated to the 6th century Cornish St Pol, a name changed later to the more familiar St Paul. Migrating to Brittany, he became Bishop of St Pol-de-Leon.

There is another legend that when builders were erecting the first church, they tried to place it on a different site, but changed their minds because every night "ghostly" forces removed the building materials to the present position nearer the River Dart.

Historian Thomas Westcote (c. 1620) wrote that Saxon King Athelstan (895–939), while uniting England, built a castle at Staverton and bestowed church and lands on Exeter's monastery. By 1244 records show that the "Dean and Chapter of Exeter Cathedral held church and manor in the gift of the King", and several clergy were stationed there.

Research suggests that an 11th century Norman church was rebuilt and enlarged in the 14th and 15th centuries.

Bishop Stapeldon's visitation report in 1314 commended the fine new mass book. The chalice "although not gilded inside was otherwise decent, but there was an old cope of little value and the altar frontal was shabby". Promising indulgences for sins, the bishop told parishioners to build

Staverton Bridge, which still affords magnificent views of the Dart.

"Sir Walter, Vicar, (parishioners said) conducts himself well and honestly and informs them well about things spiritual. His Vicarage is worth 10 marks."

The long association with the Rowes, lords of the manor, is recalled in a brass memorial to John Rowe, Sergeant at Law of Totnes, died 1592, aged 82. The epitaph to his descendant John Rowe, High Sheriff of Devon, recorded his death "on ye 17th day of November, 1688, aged 73 years and more".

John Prince, of Berry Pomeroy, wrote in *Worthies of Devon* that John had been made sheriff by James II because he was a Roman Catholic, but that he died the same year – "Tis supposed his honour hastened his death in fear of what might ensue" (when the King went into exile).

Among other well-known families were the Goulds, one of whom married Margaret Dunning, of Ashburton. Her distinctive epitaph reads: "Death darts at all, spares not a Margaret; although a pearl on Go(u)ld most richly set."

When in 1875 "the church was unroofed and had been disused many months", the Rev H. T. Atherley spent large sums in repairs.

Some Gould family memorials thrown out in the process were claimed by historian Sabine Baring-Gould and placed in his own Lewtrenchard Church. He did, however, give Staverton a fine candelabra, which came from Mechelen Cathedral (Belgium).

The beautiful old screen, expertly restored, now has the figure of Christ in glory given by Edward Drake-Brockman (Vicar 1922–57) in memory of his wife. Four mediaeval bells were recast into a ring of six by Bilbie of Cullompton in 1766.

ST MARY'S CHURCH, DARTINGTON

STANDING with Gothic grace beside the main road, the Church of St Mary, Dartington, looks strangely unweathered to the many visitors who pass on the way to the celebrated Dartington Hall.

The reason is that the church was erected in 1880 to replace the mediaeval building, which was situated beside the great manor itself on the hill overlooking the Dart River. The old church was taken down in 1873, but the tower remains as part of the Dartington Hall buildings, thought to have been mainly the creation of a Royal Duke of Exeter, who had made this his principal home 600 years ago.

Monuments have been kept intact in the old church tower in honour of the Champernowne family, who acquired the estate in the 16th century. One commemorates Sir Arthur Champernowne, who in 1563 was one of the two MPs for Totnes Borough, just downstream from Dartington.

The family has deep roots in Devon history at Modbury, Filleigh, and Atherington, but it was a

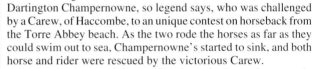

Dartington Champernowne, so legend says, who was challenged by a Carew, of Haccombe, to an unique contest on horseback from the Torre Abbey beach. As the two rode the horses as far as they could swim out to sea, Champernowne's started to sink, and both horse and rider were rescued by the victorious Carew.

So the story goes, and for proof, their rusting horseshoes remain nailed to Haccombe Church door to this day.

Champernownes lived at Dartington until early in the 20th century, but by 1925, when the Elmhirsts bought the hall, the buildings were in a sorry state. Their subsequent restoration is a story in itself.

Three members of the Froude family, whose father, Archdeacon Froude, was Rector of Dartington for 60 years, played prominent roles in Victorian England. J. A. Froude's *History of England* and many other works are remembered for their "engaging style".

R. A. Froude was a leading member of the Oxford tractarian (high church) movement; and brother William made his name in scientific research after being an assistant to Brunel.

Dartington is now rightly famous for the elegance of its restored buildings, its "environmental" shops and restaurants, and as a centre for innovative crafts and artistic and musical activity.

There may also be a spiritual quality in the peaceful air – persuading Prof C. E. M. Joad, of radio and television fame, to exchange atheism for Christian belief. One of his stated reasons was the dogged determination of country clergy in proclaiming the faith in the face of strong opposition and indifference.

The "new" Dartington church's light and lovely interior houses the font, screen, and pulpit rescued from the older building. The altar was constructed out of ancient timbers replaced during repairs to the roof of the great hall.

ST THOMAS OF CANTERBURY CHURCH, KINGSWEAR

CENTURIES ago Kingswear citizens dug into the steep hillside to provide a base for their church, which overlooks the historic stretch of water to Dartmouth.

Later, two castles were built on either side of the entrance to the natural harbour formed by the River Dart. They were raised on the two headlands as a precaution after French ships raided Dartmouth 500 years ago.

If the enemy did manage to pass through the castles' bombardment, they came up against an iron chain which was drawn up across the water in times of danger.

The fascinating weather-beaten tombstone which now resides safely within the church was dug up from the graveyard more than 250 years ago, according to Dean Milles of Exeter, writing in 1755. The inscription in ancient French can still be just deciphered, and the translation reads: "You come here to pray for the soul of Philip – 30 days pardon will be your reward."

It is thought that Philip was a 13th century priest who was stationed here.

The French connection was dramatically renewed in the Second World War, when Charles de Gaulle established headquarters at Kingswear.

Built by Kingwear's squire and patron, William De Vasci, the church was one of the earliest dedicated to St Thomas, martyr, murdered in Canterbury Cathedral in 1170.

It was the venue for an historic convocation in 1273, when Bishop Bronescombe met five citizens of Okehampton, whose actions in raiding graveyard vaults had led to their church being closed and the people excommunicated. The bishop lifted the ban when the men agreed to pay a fine of 100s (£5).

The tower has stood for 600 years, and the 14th century font of Purbeck marble was restored after spending time as a garden ornament. Two of the three mediaeval bells have been retained, the other being sold in 1767 to buy a clock.

Maintained to this day as a residence, Kingswear Castle was fortified by Royalist Sir Henry Cary, of Cockington, but captured by the Roundheads under General Thomas Fairfax in 1646.

Memorials record the courage of two men with local connections. One dispays the citation for the Victoria Cross won on 28 May 1982, in the Falklands, by Lt Col Herbert Jones of the Parachute Regiment.

The other tells how Thomas Short, aged 65, a mason, dived into Kingswear Cove on 22 June 1871 to save Sarah Ellis from drowning and lost his own life as a consequence. The tablet was erected by two men who "witnessed his noble conduct".

At Brookhill, an old house near the castle, is a mantelpiece brought from Greenway House, further up the Dart, where Sir Walter Raleigh stayed with his cousins, the Gilberts. Its significance lies in the story that Sir Walter puffed the first pipe of tobacco ever smoked in England with his elbow resting on this very shelf!

Rightly or wrongly, some still recite the jingle: "When Kingswear was a market town, Dartmouth was a fuzzy down."

ST PETROC'S CHURCH, HARFORD

STANDING at the entrance to Dartmoor in the spectacular valley of the River Erme, the ancient parish church of Harford is dedicated to the 6th century Cornish saint Petroc, founder of many places of worship in the West Country.

A window depicts St Petroc and St Hubert standing on either side of Christ; both were associated with the hunting scene. Petroc is said to have saved a stag from the hounds and to have converted the huntsman, Constantine, whose name is perpetuated in a bay near Padstow.

A tradition asserts that St Hubert, an 8th century missionary in the Ardennes, was converted during a hunt when he met a stag with a cross between its antlers. Perversely, perhaps, he has been named as the patron saint of huntsmen.

A church may have been established here in Petroc's time. Rescued from a garden in the 20th century and restored to the present building is a font, possibly of Saxon origin.

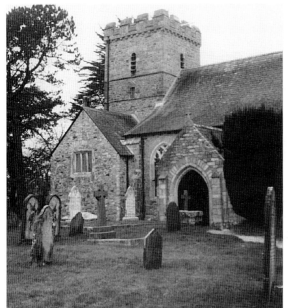

Other old features are the fine carved roof and the tower, housing three bells. Two, now cracked, were made in Exeter 600 years ago; the third, still in use, was recast in 1686 by Mordecai Cockey of Totnes.

Known as "Hereforda", meaning in Anglo-Saxon "army ford", in King Canute's time, the parish was then owned by Ordulf, "a notable thane", whose signature was on the document appointing Leofric as the first Bishop of Exeter.

First named rector was Robert de Kyllebiri.

Speaker of the House of Commons in 1563, Thomas Williams was brought up in a parish manor and is portrayed in armour on a brass memorial, with the inscription: "The common peace he studied to preserve, and true religion ever to maintain".

When another local lad, John Prideaux, applied unsuccessfully to become parish clerk in the neighbouring parish of Ugborough, a sympathetic patron gave him a scholarship to Exeter College, Oxford.

His career blossomed as chaplain to King James I and then to Charles I, and in 1641 he became Bishop of Worcester – all because (as he was wont to say) he failed to be appointed a parish clerk.

The family monument in the church shows his father, also John, with his wife and 10 children, the boy in the red robes of a doctor of divinity representing Bishop John. All are kneeling at a priedieu – perhaps a subtle pun on their name.

A member of another famous local family, Elizabeth Chudleigh, was patroness of the church in 1766. Later, as Duchess of Kingston, she was tried in London for bigamy, following a dispute over her husband's will. The prosecutor was the celebrated Devon lawyer John Dunning, first Lord Ashburton.

William Hart, rector from 1633 to 1666 during the Commonwealth, suffered much from raids by Roundhead soldiers, but was "preserved in his living" by the goodwill of "local gentlemen" until the monarchy was restored.

Victorian restoration became essential after a report in 1860 that "two large jackdaws in the tower, like imprisoned souls, were trying to break the west window". Both church and churchyard are now a credit to their delightful setting.

ST MARY THE VIRGIN CHURCH, HOLNE

GATEWAY to south Dartmoor and guardian of the fairest stretch of the River Dart, Holne village clusters around its ancient inn below the church, which stands on a spectacular height overlooking a wide area of rural Devon.

Remains of an Iron Age fort and the discovery of old British, as well as Greek and Roman currency are signs that the parish was inhabited from earliest times.

Known as "Holla" (from the holly trees in the Chase) in the Domesday survey, church, village, and lands were in the care of Norman landlords, including William de Falaise, Philip de Columbers, and finally the Bourchiers, whose descendants, the Wreys, were resident until the 19th century.

The lord of South Holne Manor in 1258 gave "100 acres of scrub" to Buckfast Abbey, which then had an interest in the church. It was said to be a typical gift of certain nobles: "Not good enough for man, so it is given to God."

Roger Prigge (1240) was the first recorded rector.

When Holne Bridge was washed away in 1413, Bishop Stafford of Exeter absolved the sins of those parishioners who contributed to its repair.

Another Bishop of Exeter, Hugh Oldham (1504–19), gave the splendid oak pulpit, displaying his own crest among others, including those of the Bourchiers and Buckfast Abbey.

The much-admired painted panels of the screen depict Christ crowning the Virgin Mary, surrounded by worshipping saints.

The old parish revel was on 1 August, Lammas Day, which is derived from "Loaf Mass", the offering of the first loaf of the new harvest. In preparation, it was the custom on Dartmoor always to cut the first sheaf, ripe or not, on 20 July.

The Dole Stone, a flat table tomb near the entrance, was used in former times to distribute gifts to the needy.

Royalist Rector Richard Kaye was ejected by the Parliamentarians and reduced to such poverty that "his wife a gentlewoman of good fortune was forced to work to support the family".

With the Restoration of King Charles II, "intruder" Gastick E. White was in turn ejected in favour of Nicholas Stephens, who was instituted on 24 December 1660 – a Merry Christmas indeed!

A window in memory of Charles Kingsley, author of *Westward Ho!* and *The Water Babies*, records that he was born and baptised here in 1819 when his father was curate. He wrote to his father on a return visit in 1849: "What I saw justifies your praise. People were full of you and welcomed me as your son."

A fading inscription on the 1780 tomb of Edward Collins, landlord of the Church House Inn, was deciphered by the Dartmoor author, William Crossing: "Here lies poor Ned, on his last mattress bed. During life he was honest and free. He knew well the Chace, but now has run his race, and his name was Collins d'ye see."

John Rowe, rector, in 1737 paid out parish money to those who displayed, on the church yew tree, brushes of the foxes they had killed.

In the latter part of the 20th century Archbishop of Canterbury Michael Ramsey and Mrs Ramsey made Holne their summer retreat, striding over the moors and finding spiritual recreation at both church and inn.

ST PETROC'S CHURCH, SOUTH BRENT

ST PETROC is the patron saint of one of Devon's finest churches at South Brent, giving rise to the belief that the Cornishman may have founded a mission chapel on this site in the 6th century, about the time when monks first created a cell at Buckfast.

The Abbot of Buckfast (the official foundation date of the abbey was 1018) had the manor and care of the church before the Norman Conquest, according to the Rev Sabine Baring-Gould.

The oldest part of the present building is the sturdy Norman tower, part of the first stone church built by the abbots, who after 1066 "held the manor of Brent of our Lord the King in pure alms", erected a gallows, and set the assize (price) of those two essentials of life – bread and beer.

On the negative side, it was claimed that the abbey enclosed a large area of the south moor, which is part of the parish of South Brent, and damaged the environment by cutting and selling peat "wherein they derived great income".

The treasured circular font, with a central theme of honeysuckle, was carved from red sandstone in those early days.

A riot in 1435 broke centuries of peaceful devotion. Vicar John Hay was at vespers on the feast of Corpus Christi, when he was removed by a violent gang and murdered in the churchyard.

Shocked by the incident, Bishop Lacy ordered a massive rebuilding of the church and dedicated

the new high altar to St Petroc and two other altars on 11 September 1436.

Sir William Petre gave his name to two parish boundary stones still standing in the heart of the south moor as proof of his acquiring the manor lands and church when Buckfast Abbey was closed in 1538. The deal was confirmed by Pope Paul IV in Queen Mary's reign, because of the Roman Catholic sympathies of the family.

Petre later shared the parish income with the Dean and Chapter of Christ Church, Oxford, but both were induced to forgo a greater part of the tithes received to improve the Vicarage living, which was "so poor as to be unable to support a fitting pastor".

A century later Royalist Vicar John Gandy was removed from the Vicarage by the Roundheads, who marched him to Dartmouth dressed in his full robes, Bible in hand. His wife and three children – one a baby a few weeks old – went with him.

Selling what remained of his books to buy groceries, the exiled vicar and his family lived first in London then in Bridport, until he was restored to South Brent when Charles II was crowned in 1660.

Between 1845 and 1920, while three generations of the Spear-Cole family were vicars, substantial repairs were made to the building, including a major restoration in 1870 at the behest of the Archdeacon of Totnes.

Brent, meaning "steep", takes its name from the 1,000ft hill above the town, from which there are magnificent views of Dartmoor and the countryside. Below, a fine cedar of Lebanon and a mighty yew adorn the peaceful setting of the churchyard.

ST PETER'S CHURCH, BUCKLAND TOUT SAINTS

BUCKLAND Tout Saints is a name which lends exotic charm to the South Hams, and it would be natural to assume that the parish church is dedicated to "All Saints". The patron is in fact St Peter.

"Bochelanda" was the name given at Domesday, and in 1197 the manor was occupied by Sanson de Cari, underlord to Richard de Lamene. Early in the 13th century the property passed to the family whose name sets it apart from the six other "Bucklands" in Devon.

Records reveal that in 1238 Lucas de "Tuz-Seinz" was granted a "furlong of land and a share of a mill". William "Tutseyn" held the manor, with one quarter of a knight's fee (to serve the King). He was succeeded by John "Toutseynz" in 1303.

The family built the first chapel close to their home, according to Victorian researcher James Davidson. Sir William Bowringe, a Vicar of Loddiswell in 1435, "took oath to maintain all necessities in the chapel of Buckland, as it was from old time wont to be constituted".

Tristram Risdon, the antiquary of St Giles-in-the-Wood, near Great Torrington, author (1605–1630) of *A Survey of the County of Devon*, used the spelling "Toutsants" and wrote that "six descendants of this name" owned the manor.

This variation may well be derived from the old French, meaning "All saints"; equally possible is the translation "All well", "sants" being the equivalent of the modern French "santé", meaning health.

The latter theory is given an interesting twist by the Rev W. Keble Martin, author and artist of the internationally acclaimed book *The Concise British Flora in Colour*. He lists under the folk name of "Tutsan" the wildflower *Hypericum androsaemum*. Known also as St John's Wort, it was used as a curative herb in mediaeval times and a related species is the basis for the reproduction of modern herbal remedies.

Whatever the original import of the parish's name, St Peter's Church has a superb position. It is a tonic for both body and mind to breathe the pure air and absorb the spectacular views on all sides.

A diocesan visitation report of 1782 records: "This chapel, which has been in ruins, was about four years since rebuilt at a little distance from the ancient site by John Henry Southcote esqr, in a style and manner which does honour to the taste and benevolence of that gentleman." It was consecrated in 1779.

At the same time Southcote built the fine Queen Anne house which now serves as the Buckland Tout Saints Hotel.

After a visit in 1841 Davidson reported that the building was "damp and neglected", and services were held only once a month. Later in the century it was fully restored, and as we enter the 21st century it is a peaceful and well-preserved place of worship.

Most South Hams parishes have good histories compiled by residents. *Buckland Tout Saints, a Parish History* by Patricia Cove and Betty Warne (160 pages) is in a class of its own for detailed research.

ST ANDREW'S CHURCH, SOUTH HUISH

THE CLOSURE in 1869 of St Andrew's Church, South Huish, which had served the inhabitants of a fair South Hams valley for many centuries, is still regarded by some as a tragedy that should never have happened.

The incumbent, the Rev Dr Alfred Earle, was also resident Vicar of West Alvington, which had been the mother church of South Huish since its consecration almost exactly 600 years earlier, by Bishop Walter Bronescombe on 1 August 1270.

But it was in his other role as Archdeacon of Totnes that Dr Earle decided St Andrew's should be closed – for two reasons.

He pointed out that because the neighbouring hamlet of Galmpton by then had more inhabitants than South Huish, it would make sense to build a new church there.

Secondly, the South Huish Church was in such a poor state of repair that members of the congregation would have to raise £300 to restore it. Writing soon after the event, historian Beatrix Cresswell claimed that it would have been difficult for the local people, who were not rich, to raise 300 shillings.

Responding to fierce local opposition to the closure, the Ecclesiastical Commissioners offered £100 a year to maintain the building, but this was blocked by Archdeacon Earle.

Miss K. M. Clarke, an expert on church furnishings of the period, wrote: "It was a wise move [to close the church], as the new building would be so much more convenient; but there was no reason that South Huish Church should have been gutted."

She was referring to the removal from the condemned building of the fine 16th century screen, sold to a relation of the archdeacon and installed in the private chapel of Bowringsleigh House in West Alvington parish.

The old font and four bells were transferred to the new church at Galmpton; granite columns were removed to the north aisle in Dodbrooke Church; and carved alabaster sculptures of the Annunciation, the Adoration of the Magi, and the Resurrection were retained by the archdeacon, who later donated them to the Devon and Exeter Institution Library in the Cathedral Close.

As a final blow to local pride, an auctioneer was hired from Kingsbridge to sell other items, including the altar, altar rails, prayer desk, pulpit, roof bosses, window glass, doors, pews, and slates and lead from the roof.

Such was the affection for "the church which had been allowed to perish" that for many years after its closure services were being held in its shell, the old sexton erecting a pile of stones on the north side of the chancel as a makeshift pulpit for officiating ministers.

When Archdeacon Earle was made a London suffragan bishop by his friend, Bishop (later Archbishop) Frederick Temple, he took the title of Bishop of Malborough from another South Hams Church which had been in his care. Finally he was made Dean of Exeter.

ST MICHAEL AND ALL ANGELS CHURCH, CORNWOOD

STANDING above its village, Cornwood Church is dedicated (as buildings on lofty locations often are) to St Michael and All Angels. The parish it serves consists of more than 10,000 acres, covering a large area of Dartmoor.

It includes the upper reaches of the Erme and Yealm Rivers, and on Stall Moor is the longest Bronze Age single stone row in the world, ascending from the Erme plains up to Green Hill. It was measured in 1880 as being 11,239ft 8in long (about $2\frac{1}{4}$ miles).

The church has a fascinating story to match its remote site and sturdy appearance, and its monuments attest a long association with some of Devon's oldest families.

Revenue from the lands of "Cornhuda" was granted after the Norman Conquest to Robert, Count of Mortain, half-brother of King William I. Early documentary evidence of a church comes in 1263, when John de Langeford was appointed rector.

A grand ceremony was recorded when Sir John Bereware was installed as rector. The church had just been restored by its patron, Sir John Dawney, and Bishop John Grandisson dedicated a new high altar and two aisle altars.

In the 14th century the Courtenays inherited the church advowson through marriage to the Dawneys.

The church did not escape the ravages of the Civil War. Vicar Henry Smith, who supported the cause of Charles I, was chased from the Vicarage with his wife and family by the Roundheads and he was later imprisoned and died at Exeter.

His Puritan successor, the Rev Walter Shute, removed all coloured glass from the church and took away the rood loft (figure of Christ crucified) from above the screen, but spared the Jacobean pulpit. He also changed his style of churchmanship sufficiently to be allowed to stay in office when Charles II was crowned.

Recalling these turbulent times is the memorial to Benjamin Burrell, which proudly proclaims that he a was a captain in Charles I's army and records his death at the age of 90 in 1715.

A window coat of arms marks the long association with the parish of the Hele family, who sprang into prominence when Sir John Hele became Sergeant-at-Law, first to Queen Elizabeth I, and later to King James I when fellow Devonian Sir Walter Raleigh was tried for treason.

It seems that the two families were sometimes on friendly terms, because a relation of Sir Walter, Carew Raleigh, sold Fardel Manor in Cornwood to the Heles.

Several memorials record the long association of the Rogers family with the parish, including a martyr, Dr John Rogers, who was burned at the stake in the reign of Queen Mary (1555).

Residing at the Domesday manor of Blachford, the Rogers had a succession of baronets and MPs from 1699, until finally one was made Lord Blachford in 1871. The spectacular marble and alabaster reredos was his gift to the church.

Kneeling figures in what is known as the Slade chapel represent Philip Cole and his wife Joane, daughter of Thomas Williams, Speaker of the House of Commons in Queen Elizabeth's reign (his memorial is in neighbouring Harford Church).

The Cholwiches, who held Cholwich Town (Farm) in the north of the parish, are remembered by a churchyard tomb. The family, whose story is told in detail in Prof Hoskins, *Old Devon*, prospered and acquired property in other parts of Devon, including Blackawton, where their

names are recorded on numerous memorials.

The churchyard tomb of Admiral Thomas Trefusis, who died in 1751, links the parish with yet another famous Devon name.

Perhaps the strangest feature is the unusually frank mural epitaph to Robert and Dorothy Bellmaine:

"Here's rest and peace within this grave,
Which in life we could never have"!

ST MARTIN'S CHURCH, SHERFORD

BEFORE the Norman Conquest there was a chapel at Sherford linked to the ancient Church of St Olave's, Exeter. Both churches were founded by Countess Gytha, widow of Earl Godwin and mother of King Harold.

A freely translated document attests: "I Countess Gytha, grant to the Church of St Olaf (and later the attached Priory of St Nicholas) my land at Scireford (Sherford Manor), which is my dower, for the eternal salvation of my soul and that of my lord Earl Godwin" (who died in 1053).

O. J. Reichel in *Domesday Churches of Devon* also lists the oratory of Sherford as being attached to St Olave's and the priory, and discloses that the Royal Sherford Manor later came into the hands of Battle Abbey.

Passing through the ivy-covered lychgate up the steps into St Martin's, visitors find a light and elegant building, rebuilt in local stone at the end of the 14th century.

In particular, the screen, which was taken down and stored for safety during the Second World War, has drawn enthusiastic comment from connoisseurs. The six figures of the apostles are praised for their artistic merit and are regarded as among the best examples of their kind in England.

A chancel gravestone and mural tablet commemorate George Reynell and his wife (died 1643 and 1662), of Malston, a Domesday property which belonged to Brictric, Thane of Gloucester, before all his lands were confiscated by William I.

Robert de Malleston acquired the manor from Ralf de Pomeroy in 1285, and Dean Milles of Exeter in his 18th century "Parochial Returns" wrote that "the Manor of Malston came to the Reynells by marriage with Elizabeth Malston."

Lord of the manor in 1413 was Walter Reynell, who would serve at Agincourt (1415).

Linked with the national past was another Domesday manor, Keynedon, home of John Hals, Justice of the Common Pleas in 1423. His son, also John Hals, who was born at the manor, was Bishop of Coventry and Lichfield from 1459 until 1490.

After visiting the church in 1841, J. Davidson in his *Church Notes* admires the pulpit, which had recently been constructed out of old woodwork carved in a distinctive Devon design.

Evidence that the fine interior of the church is appreciated by today's parishioners is found in their tapestry work of the hassocks and altar kneeler, and right up to date is the Millennium Book, *One Thousand Years of Sherford* (92 pages), by J. R. Goodman.

ST MARY'S CHURCH, WOODLEIGH

A COMMUNITY devoted to farming the rolling South Hams countryside has supported the Church of St Mary, Woodleigh, over the centuries. In these days of remorseless development in "green" areas, long may it remain that way.

A question is sometimes asked why so pleasantly remote a parish (population in AD 2000 was 131) should lend its name to the large Woodleigh Deanery, which comprises 30 parishes, serving a population of some 25,000.

Apart from its central position, one possible answer is the early possession of Woodleigh lands by members of the influential Courtenay and Fortescue families.

Significant, too, is the fact that the Domesday manor "Odelia" was held by one Robert de Albemarla. There may be a family connection here with General Monk, a native of Merton in North Devon, who was responsible for restoring the Stuarts to the throne in the person of Charles II. He was rewarded with the title of the 1st Duke of Albemarle.

In 1243 Rolf de Alba Marla held the manor lands from the Courtenays (Earls of Devon), who maintained the right to appoint rectors to the church.

The Courtenays' under tenant in 1383 was Sir Peter de Fishacre, who was also squire of the neighbouring parish of Moreleigh. It was during a quarrel about tithes that Sir Peter resorted to violence and killed the Rector of Woodleigh.

News of the murder reached Rome, and the squire was ordered by the Pope to rebuild the Church of All Saints at Moreleigh to atone for his wicked deed (see page 30).

Woodleigh Church has a 12th century font, but the most admired feature is the Easter sepulchre built by a more fortunate rector, the Rev Thomas Smythe, who was instituted on 9 March 1492, on the presentation of Edward Courtenay, Marquis of Exeter.

The sepulchre is finely sculptured and has been described as the finest of its kind in Exeter Diocese. The work, which bears the rector's initials TS, was probably completed c 1500 – well before his death in 1527.

A mural nave tablet to Peter Fortescue represents the long association with the parish of the family who occupied "La Wode" manor. In 1420 Bishop Lacy gave permission for Henry and Catherine Fortescue to build a private chapel there.

The parish register was brightened by the frank contributions of the Rev Walter Efford during his 52 years as rector from 1676 to 1728.

"I, Walter Efford, was inducted to the Rectory of Woodleigh 29th July, 1676, by Mr Henry Warren, Vicar of Loddiswell, and after seven years unduly being kept out by Dr Fulford, Archdeacon of Totnes, and Mr Binmore, a non-conforming minister, in my wrong, to divide the profits. Fulford, being incumbent, shuffled off his resignation until the time of my enforced admittance."

In his capacity as the Rural Dean of Woodleigh, Mr Efford listed the contributions made by the South Hams parishes for the rebuilding of St Paul's Cathedral after the Great Fire of London – a grand total of £16 4s 5d (£16.22).

On 28 August 1686, he wrote: "There was given by Lady Amy Fortescue, relict of Sir Peter Fortescue, baronet, a large silver flagon to be forever used in the celebration of Holy Communion in this parish of Woodleigh of the Holy Sacrament, and never to be alienated nor profaned for common use."

ST JOHN THE EVANGELIST CHURCH, IVYBRIDGE

"DELIGHTFULLY situated on the Erme, one of the most beautiful of the Dartmoor rivers, the large village of Ivybridge extends itself into four parishes, and these meet at the structure (bridge) which gives the place its name."

So wrote William Crossing in his classic *Guide to Dartmoor* nearly a hundred years ago. His liking for Ivybridge may have been influenced by the fact that he married Emma Witheridge, a girl from the village, in 1872, and they settled in South Brent, a few miles to the east on the Plymouth–Exeter road.

For long centuries Ivybridge was "a place that admits a great through fare", according to Tristram Risdon writing around 1605. Bridges were undoubtedly constructed here from earliest times to enable traffic to cross the river on the main route to the Southwest.

In King Edward I's reign (1272–1307) land tenure was granted to the suitably named Alfred de Ponte Hedera, but the area was sparsely populated and, unless he had a private chapel, Alfred probably worshipped at the parish Church of St Michael and All Angels, Cornwood.

The other three ecclesiastical parishes with boundaries meeting Cornwood at the bridge were Harford, Ermington, and Ugborough.

First mention of a church at Ivybridge was as a chapel-at-ease of Cornwood parish c.1400. A building on this site was rededicated on 5 October 1835, after extension and alterations. Writing in his survey of Devon churches a few years later, James Davidson described the chapel-at-ease as large and without any architectural pretensions.

Near the close of the 19th century the building was struck with lightning and soon became a spectacular ruin covered in ivy. The new church was erected alongside it in 1882, when the parish was separated from Cornwood.

Among the furnishings removed from the old building was a memorial with an inscription which again demonstrated Devon's close links with the sea: "Commander Robert Heron Burton RN who with his brave fellow officers and men perished in the wreck of HMS *Orpheus* off the West Coast of New Zealand on 7th February 1863 in his 34th year. This tablet was erected by his widow."

Regarded as the southern gateway of Dartmoor (corresponding to Okehampton 24 miles away on the northern border), Ivybridge developed from a 19th century village into a market town, and is now a growing centre of population of more than 10,000 citizens. St John's Parish Church is the centre of a Rural Deanery covering nine benefices and 16 churches on both sides of the A38 main highway.

Besides the parish church, the people are served by Methodist, Congregational, Baptist, and two Community Churches in the town itself, and by a Roman Catholic Church at St Austin's Priory, Cadeleigh, nearby.

In a lively ecumenical atmosphere, young people are well catered for by youth clubs and uniformed organisations.

When I visited St John's, the walls were covered with posters made for a festival by Ivybridge school pupils.

Local people insist that while the town's population may be growing, the friendly village atmosphere remains.

ST LEONARD'S CHURCH, HALWELL

BUILT of local stone and set neatly into a hillside near a main route to Dartmouth, St Leonard's, Halwell, modestly maintains its traditional role as the spiritual centre of a small local community.

There is now no obvious sign that Halwell was chosen by King Alfred in the late 9th century as one of the four Devon burhs, or fortified camps, standing at the head of estuaries (in Halwell's case Dartmouth and Kingsbridge) to withstand repeated Danish invasions.

Two of the four burhs – Exeter and Lydford – maintained their status, but by the time of the Norman Conquest, Halwell had been replaced by Totnes and Pilton by Barnstaple.

Alfred's original choice of Halwell was influenced by the proximity of not one, but two Iron Age forts in the area – one which gives the village of Halwell (short for "Holy well") its name. The other, more extensive, excavation at Stanborough overlooks a wide area and also gave its name to a Saxon "hundred" or legal and taxation centre reaching down to the coast.

This earlier importance was beginning to be a distant memory when the first Norman church was built here and dedicated to St Leonard, the hermit who was a favourite of crusaders returning to Germany and England from the Holy Land.

After the Conquest the parish came under the patronage of Judhael of Totnes, and first reference to the church was made in records of 1288. By 1536 it was described as a chapel in the care of the clergy of Harberton church.

The building remains a quiet haven with pleasant old box pews and a reredos of pale blue and white freestone.

One mural memorial in particular catches the eye, with the heading "In memory of the progeny of Thomas Elford Sheriff of Cornwall 1301." His descendants at Longthorne Manor, a father and son, both christened William, are commemorated in rhyme:

"Both lie beneath this stone,
Our souls, our flesh, our bone,
Rest on the corner stone.
Here lie I consumed and unseen.
Yea now, I am as if I had not been;
From Earthly mother from her dyeing womb,
To Earth my mother to another tomb."

The imperial call from overseas reached this corner of Devon, with two memorials to men who served in the "Hon East India Company".

Captain R. E. Goodrich of the company's navy died at sea aged 47 in 1833; he was remembered by a monument "raised by an attached wife and tender mother".

Major General Hilley, of Stanborough "in this parish", also of the East India Company, died in Exeter and was buried in Halwell in 1831.

When visiting this lovely building I found a pamplet issued by the Open Churches Trust, proclaiming a worthy purpose "to open the many locked churches to enable the public to use them and enjoy their beauty and history".

CHURCH OF THE BLESSED VIRGIN MARY, RATTERY

FINDING a church in most Devon villages is not difficult. In Rattery it is the spire of the Parish Church of St Mary the Virgin which catches the eye, and as visitors approach it down a peaceful lane, their attention is diverted by a plaque on the whitewashed wall of an attractive building on the left.

It reads: "Church House Inn AD 1020", giving a clue to the antiquity of this parish, which in 1088 after the Norman Conquest was bestowed on William de Falaise as "Lord of Rattreu". His father at the time of the Conquest had secured land at Cameis in Pembrokeshire, where he established Dogmael Abbey.

According to early records, the abbey was given "The Manor of Rattreu in England" in 1116. This was confirmed by a 1244 document that "The Abbot of Cameis holds Rattreu".

Dr G. Oliver in his *Ecclesiastical Antiquities of Devon* (1840) wrote that St Dogmael was a Celtic saint working in Pembrokeshire in the 6th century who later retired to Brittany. It was said that monks from the abbey built Rattery church for tenants of the manor lands, probably replacing an earlier chapel.

The circular redstone font of lotus leaf design was installed about that time. A tower was built in the 13th century.

Pembroke abbots appointed vicars at Rattery until the time of the Reformation, when the manor was sold to the Savery family, who were wealthy merchants at Totnes.

The wording on a memorial tablet confirms the family's long connection with Rattery: "The Revd. William Savery (born 1722, died 1781) ... whose ancestors lived in this parish and are buried in the chancel ... erected by his grandson William Cotton of Leatherhead Surrey".

The 15th century screen was repaired in 1911 by Miss E. R. Pinwill, one of the seven daughters of the Vicar of Ermington, whose carving skills adorn many churches in the South Hams and throughout Devon. Miss Pinwill established a church furnishing firm in Plymouth.

The cost of repairs to the screen were met by Misses Beatrix and Elizabeth Carew, of Haccombe, in the Teign Valley. The Carews entered the parish life when Sir Henry Carew married Miss Palk, heiress of Rattery manor. Family interest continues, as Sir Rivers Carew, jointly with the Bishop of Exeter, has the gift of the church living of South Brent and Rattery.

Gravestones in the south aisle record the burials of Thomas Pyne "Doctor of Physic" (1745), and his son Arthur Pyne Barrister at Law (1760).

A newspaper cutting of 1853 quoted a Mr Thomas Parnell, "an old mason", as saying that 60 years previously he had been ordered by a Mr Palk, churchwarden, to plaster over a gravestone to a member of the Pyne family, from whom Mr Palk had bought the manor. Apparently the stone carried information he wished to conceal!

A list of incumbents includes William de Pembroke (Rector 1238), who was also a chaplain at Cockington (in Torquay), which was bought from the Abbot of Dogmael by the Abbot of Torre.

More recently the Rev John Jago was Vicar for 54 years until 1954, when he died at the age of 84.

As an item of curiosity, a Victorian list of "dos and don'ts" for worshippers has been retained on the wall near the south porch entrance, including the advice: "Do not whisper to your neighbour."

ALL SAINTS CHURCH, MORELEIGH

SET apart from the through road, All Saints, Moreleigh, has a pleasing interior to match its peaceful setting. The font etablishes the building's antiquity as a home of worship, and the 18th century pulpit complete with sounding board immediately catches the eye.

Like other parish churches in the locality, it has its own romantic history.

Sir Peter Fishacre, who lived in the reign of Edward I (1272–1307), owned lands in both Moreleigh and the neighbouring parish of Woodleigh and left an indelible mark on both places.

The story goes that because he had murdered the Rector of Woodleigh in a quarrel over tithes, he was ordered by the Pope to build the church at Moreleigh as an act of penance.

Evidence of Sir Peter's connection with All Saints Church, Moreleigh, is found in a document which reveals that in 1279 he appointed a rector of the church he was supposed to have built, but there is a record of a previous rector in 1264.

This suggests that Peter Fishacre, instead of building a new church at Moreleigh, was ordered by the Pope to repair and extend a building already in existence. The ancient Norman font and the Early English style of the tower have been cited as evidence of this earlier building.

In mediaeval times there was a superstitous wish to be buried within the walls of a church, and more especially in the sanctuary, in the hope of preferential treatment in the Day of Judgement.

Sir Peter's act of murder precluded him from such benefit, according to the Devon historian Tristram Risdon, who recorded that the squire "lieth buried in the wall arched over" – that is, not in the church itself, but in a wall jutting out into the churchyard.

A similar "exclusion" rumour grew up around the tomb of Bishop Hugh Oldham, who was buried in a recess outside his own chapel in Exeter Cathedral, because (it was alleged) the Pope excommunicated him after he had quarrelled with the Abbot of Tavistock.

Oldham's biographer, Dr A. A. Mumford, throws doubt on this account, saying that the bishop, with his usual humility, had asked to be buried, not in the chapel itself, but outside its precincts.

Moreleigh has an earlier claim to historic fame, again according to Risdon, as being appointed (in succession to Diptford) the centre of the "hundred" or late Saxon and Norman legal and administrative base of a wide area extending down to the coast.

Risdon wrote: "Moreleigh may not be silenced seeing of an old fort now no better than a heap of stones, called by the name of Stanborough from when the hundred hath its name".

Halwell parish, it has been noted, also lays claim to this Iron Age fort of Stanborough.

It is always humbling to learn how much we owe to the dedicated service of past generations. The inscription on the memorial of George Langmead Hallett, churchwarden and sexton 1906–1960, records how he "devoted much of his life to the upkeep of this church".

Going back to the 18th century, William Jackson, organist of Exeter Cathedral, who won national fame as a composer, wrote in his autobiography: "Of my family I know nothing but that for many generations they were farmers at Moreleigh, an obscure place in the south-west of Devon".

ST ANDREW'S CHURCH, HARBERTON

BY GENERAL consent one of Devon's loveliest churches, St Andrew's, Harberton, also abounds in historical interest.

Its origin as a place of worship goes back to Saxon times, as the shaft of the churchyard cross testifies. Carved out of red sandstone, the font is also very early, possibly c. 1080. Some experts discern that it has a Saxon cord design and they lavish praise on its "Byzantine ornament" (or finely decorated style).

After the Norman Conquest the church came under the patronage of the Canons of Salisbury Cathedral, but in 1245 Bishop William Brewer agreed with the Bishop of Salisbury that it should be assigned to the Canons of Exeter Cathedral, who conscientiously started the process of rebuilding and extension.

It was recorded at the time: "The chancel is newly built in sumptuous manner by the (Exeter) chapter".

Visitors standing in the nave are advised to look up to admire the magnificent 14th century barrel roof, "aglow with painted beams and golden bosses", as one writer has described it.

The screen has a story of its own. While it was being repaired during the 19th century, the old picture panels were removed and replaced by new ones painted on metallic zinc by a cerain Mrs Pendarves.

A critic wrote: "Her choice of subject was guided by no historical or ecclesiastical knowledge". The contemporary historian who was also Rector of Lewtrenchard, the Rev Sabine Baring-Gould, claimed that the paintings were portraits of young ladies of the congregation in 1870, and the church guide adds: "The faces on the central gates are alleged to have been based on the daughters of a former vicar".

Rescued from a long dusty storage, some of the original panels can now be seen encased in glass on the north wall of the nave.

The names of old Devon families, including Risdon and Trist, are to be found on memorials, and a tablet was erected to Ralph Barnes, Archdeacon of Totnes and Canon residentiary of Exeter Cathedral and "Vicar of this parish where for 40 years he resided in the discharge of his duty".

The archdeacon, who died at the Vicarage and was buried in Exeter Cathedral, was however also Vicar of Heavitree in Exeter and Rector of Bratton Clovelly. While he preferred to live at Harberton, like other church leaders of his time, out of incomes received, he employed curates to officiate in his absence in the other parishes.

The Lady Chapel window commemorates Major Farquarson V.C., who lived at Dundridge.

There is an effigy of Robert Godfrey Harvey, known as Tito, who died at the age of 10. Born in Peru, his mother's homeland, he was the son of Sir Robert and Lady Harvey, who lived at Dundridge House from the end of the 19th century.

Sir Robert donated the church clock, and a charming children's corner was designed by Sybil Lady Harvey in June 1938.

When he visited the church in the 1930s, Arthur Mee remarked on a churchyard notice: "No smoking or dogs". A prophetic warning, surely, of the dangers of nicotine.

ST JAMES THE LESS CHURCH, KINGSTON

KINGSTON, as its name implies, was a Royal foundation in the time of Ethelwulf, who was King of Wessex from 839 until 858.

Probably as a defence against endless raids by the heathen Danes, the Christian ruler in the early days of his reign kept watch over the fair coastline bordering Bigbury Bay lying east of the Erme River estuary. Kingston was established as a headquarters.

Little is known of Ethelwulf, except that he won a great victory against the Danish hordes on an unidentified battleground called Aclea. He was succeeded as the King of Wessex by four sons. Ethelbald, who also married his father's widow, reigned from 858 to 860; Ethelbert (third son) from 860 to 866; Ethelred (fourth son) from 866 to 871; and finally the fifth and youngest, Alfred the Great, was King from 871 to 899.

There is every reason to believe that King Ethelwulf's Saxon subjects established the first chapel at Kingston, to thank God for being stationed in such a beautiful place, and when the occasion arose, to offer prayers before going into combat with the invading Vikings.

From the time of the Norman Conquest (and perhaps earlier) Kingston was linked ecclesiastically with Ermington, which was the adminstrative centre for a "hundred", situated a little further inland beside the River Erme. Both parishes came under the care of the Peverell family, who from their spacious acres also endowed Montacute Priory in Somerset.

The original patroness of the two churches, Matilda Peverell, between 1119 and 1129 founded the small Kerswell Priory (in the East Devon parish of Broadhembury), dependent on Montacute.

A new Kingston church was built of local stone in the early 14th century, but parishioners could not be buried there. When anybody died, it meant a tedious trek to Ermington churchyard, and eventually a plea was made to Pope Boniface himself for "the right of sepulture". Permission for a graveyard was obtained in 1401/2, but there were conditions.

Kingston residents were required to help financially in the upkeep of the "mother" Church of Ermington and attend its Festival of Dedication (5 February) and the festival days of the patron saints, St Peter and St Paul.

Set on a hill above its settlement, St James the Less has a 15th century granite font and in the sanctuary an ancient priest's chair with carved ends. One observer identified the remains of a stove on the south side of the tower used for the ceremonial kindling of the Easter candle.

In his tour of Devon parishes (c.1755) Dean Milles reported: "Service is performed here once a Sunday alternately with Ermington. Besides which they give the Curate of Ringmore £3 12s to preach and read prayers once a month. A part of the great tithes are payable to a ruined chapel, named Ockenbury, in the parish of Ringmore adjoining."

The Ven R. H. Froude, 60 years Vicar of Dartington, also pursued his other duties as Archdeacon of Totnes with zeal. After an official inspection in 1824, he ordered necessary work to be done in the church, which was "in a poor state of repair".

This proved a temporary measure, and a restoration campaign initiated in 1891 culminated in a memorable ceremonial reopening by the Bishop of Exeter, Edward Bickersteth, in 1893.

The long association with Ermington came to an end in 1934, when Kingston Church was linked with Ringmore. Both these parishes later became part of the group of eight churches centred on Modbury.